Air Power

AC-130J GHOSTRIDER

MEGAN COOLEY PETERSON

BLACK RABBIT BOOKS

Bolt is published by Black Rabbit Books
P.O. Box 3263, Mankato, Minnesota, 56002.
www.blackrabbitbooks.com

Jennifer Besel & Marysa Storm, editors;
Grant Gould, designer; Omay Ayres,
photo researcher

Library of Congress Cataloging-in-Publication Data
Names: Peterson, Megan Cooley, author.
Title: AC-130J Ghostrider / by Megan Cooley Peterson.
Description: Mankato, Minnesota : Black Rabbit Books, [2020] | Series: Bolt. Air power | Includes bibliographical references and index. | Audience: Age: 8-12. | Audience: Grade: 4-6.
Identifiers: LCCN 2018026755 (print) | LCCN 2018038245 (ebook) | ISBN 9781680727913 (e-book) | ISBN 9781680727852 (library binding) | ISBN 9781644660089 (paperback)
Subjects: LCSH: Spectre (Gunship)—Juvenile literature.
Classification: LCC UG1242.G85 (ebook) | LCC UG1242.G85 P48 2020 (print) | DDC 623.74/63—dc23
LC record available at https://lccn.loc.gov/2018026755

Printed in the United States. 1/19

Image Credits

af.mil: Airman Kai White/US Air Force, 26–27; Senior Airman Julianne Showalter/US Air Force, 20–21; US Air Force, 6 (t), 13 (bl, tl, & tr), 14–15, 32; US Air Force/Staff Sgt. Christopher Callaway, 13 (br); airman.dodlive.mil/: Master Sgt. Jack Braden, Cover; Alamy: AB Forces News Collection, 6 (b), 14, 16 (t); dpa picture alliance, 9; c-130.net: Lockheed Martin, 12 (tr); commons.wikimedia.org: SpecialOps-Guy 1, 1; af.mil, SrA Ali Flisek/US Air Force, 25; flightsim.com: Bluebaron, 28–29; hurlburt.af.mil: Senior Airman Jeff Parkinson/ US Air Force, 22; Senior Airman Jeff Parkinson/US Air Force, 3, 10–11; nationalmuseum.af.mil: US Air Force, 12 (tl); Shutterstock: inspired-fiona, 19 (bkgd); simpleplanes.com: GreenGiraffeAero-space, 12–13 (bkgd); Scriefers, 31; tacairnet.com, Raytheon, 16 (b), 17; the-blueprints.com: The Blueprints, 18–19, 26 (t); TSGT Bill Thompson/US Air Force, 4–5; wpafb.af.mil: US Air Force, 27 (b)

Every effort has been made to contact copyright holders for material reproduced in this book. Any omissions will be rectified in subsequent printings if notice is given to the publisher.

CONTENTS

CHAPTER 1

TESTING the Limits

It was a January day in 2014. An AC-130J Ghostrider sat on the runway. The new gunship was about to take its first flight.

The Ghostrider raced down the runway. Then it lifted into the sky. The pilot slowed the plane. Then he sped it up. At every speed, the plane handled well.

A Powerful Gunship

The Ghostrider is a heavily armed gunship. It carries **cannons**, **missiles**, and bombs. It's used to protect soldiers on the ground. Some people call it the ultimate battle plane.

The plane has more weapons than any other U.S. gunship.

CHAPTER 2

HISTORY of the AC-130J Ghostrider

The Ghostrider belongs to the AC-130 family of gunships. The first AC-130s were built in the 1960s. The U.S. Air Force used them in the **Vietnam War**.

THE AC-130 FLEET

AC-130H Spectre

AC-130U Spooky

AC-130W Stinger II

AC-130J Ghostrider

maximum distance without refueling

RF 4619

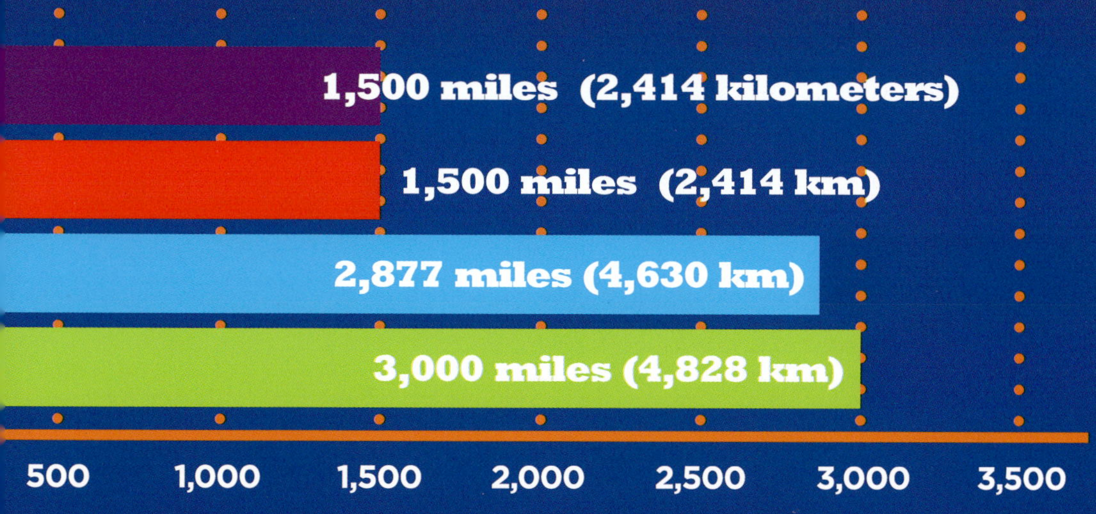
1,500 miles (2,414 kilometers)
1,500 miles (2,414 km)
2,877 miles (4,630 km)
3,000 miles (4,828 km)
500
1,000
1,500
2,000
2,500
3,000
3,500

In the future, the Ghostrider might carry a high-energy laser.

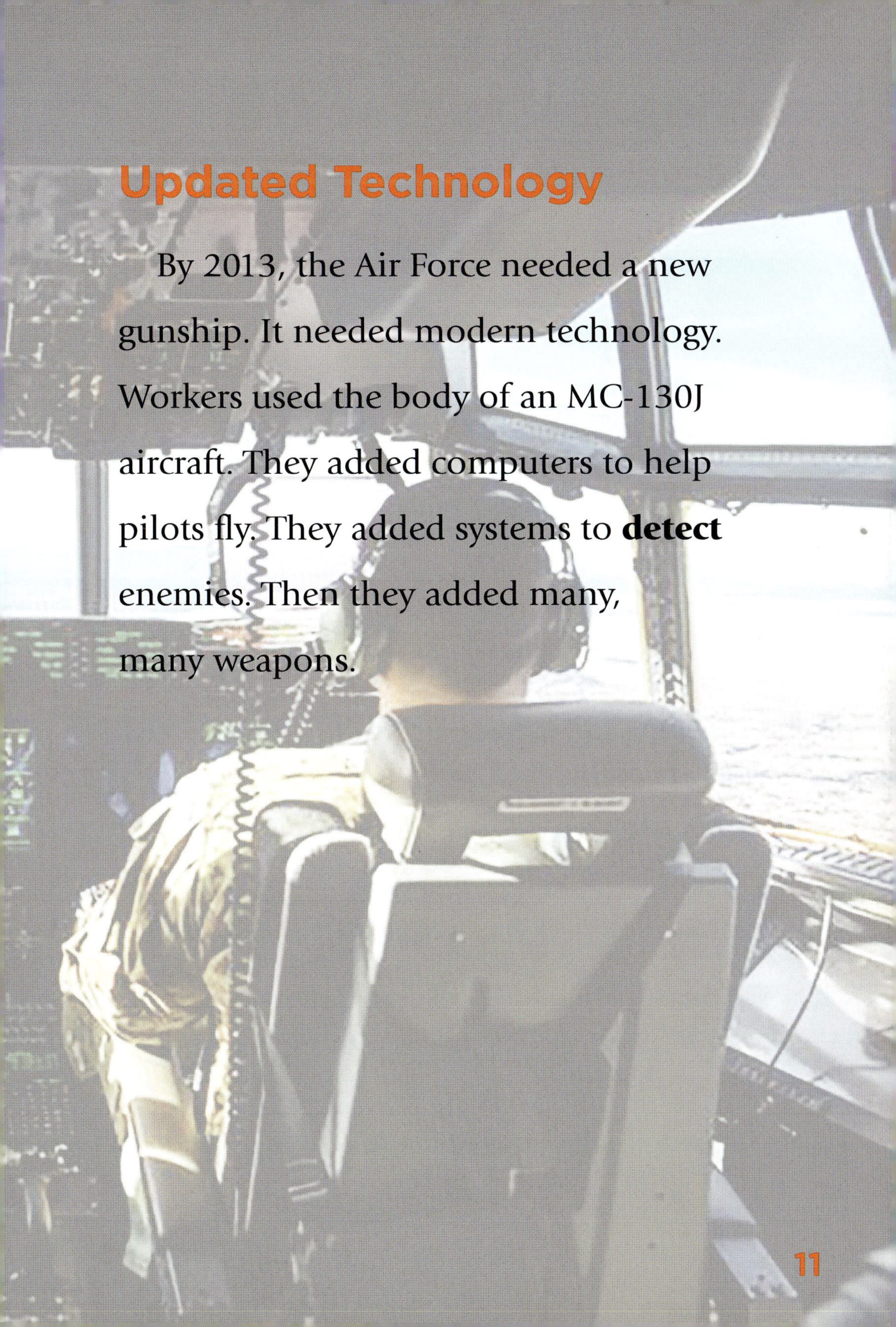

Updated Technology

By 2013, the Air Force needed a new gunship. It needed modern technology. Workers used the body of an MC-130J aircraft. They added computers to help pilots fly. They added systems to **detect** enemies. Then they added many, many weapons.

GHOSTRIDER TIMELINE

1967
The first AC-130 gunship is used in Vietnam.

2013
An MC-130J arrives at Elgin Air Force Base. Over the next year, it is changed into the AC-130J.

1965

2012
The AC-130J is named Ghostrider.

2015

The Air Force adds a 105mm cannon to the Ghostrider.

2019 or 2020

Crews hope to be ready to use the planes in **combat**.

2014

The Ghostrider completes its first test flight.

2018

Officials say the plane is combat ready. Pilots start training with it.

CHAPTER 3

The AC-130J Ghostrider FEATURES

The Ghostrider is one of the deadliest gunships flying today. It has two cannons. The 105mm cannon fires 10 shells per minute. The 30mm cannon shoots 200 bullets per minute.

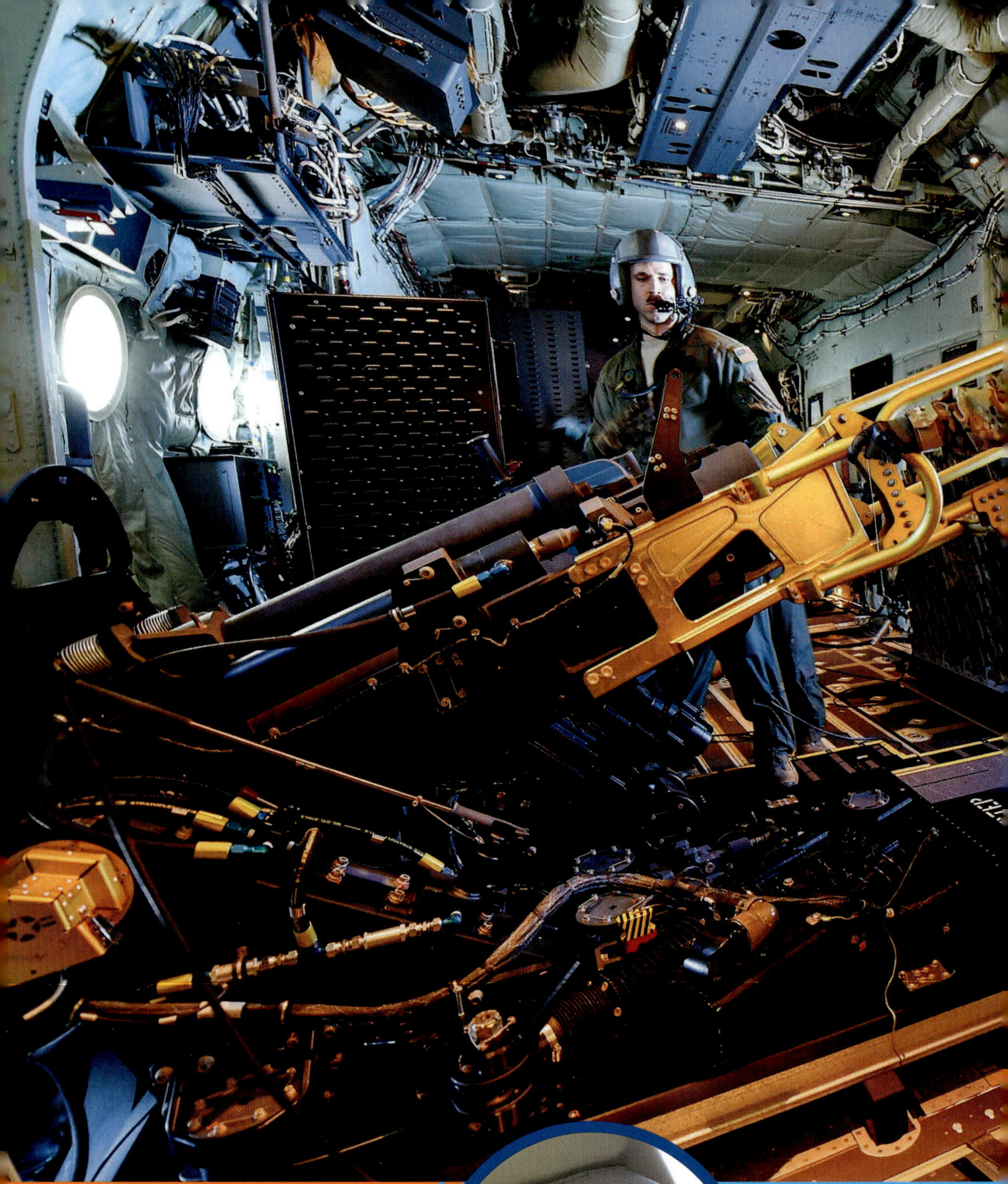

Some of the Ghostrider's Weapons

AGM-176A Griffin missile

Bombs and Missiles

The plane also carries up to 42,000 pounds (19,051 kilograms) of bombs and missiles. Bombs drop from the plane's wings. **GPS** and lasers guide weapons to their targets.

GBU-39 **small diameter bomb**

Technology

The Ghostrider blasts into battle with the latest technology. **Radar** and **sensors** track enemy aircraft. They warn pilots of incoming attacks. A computer inside the cargo bay controls the plane's weapons.

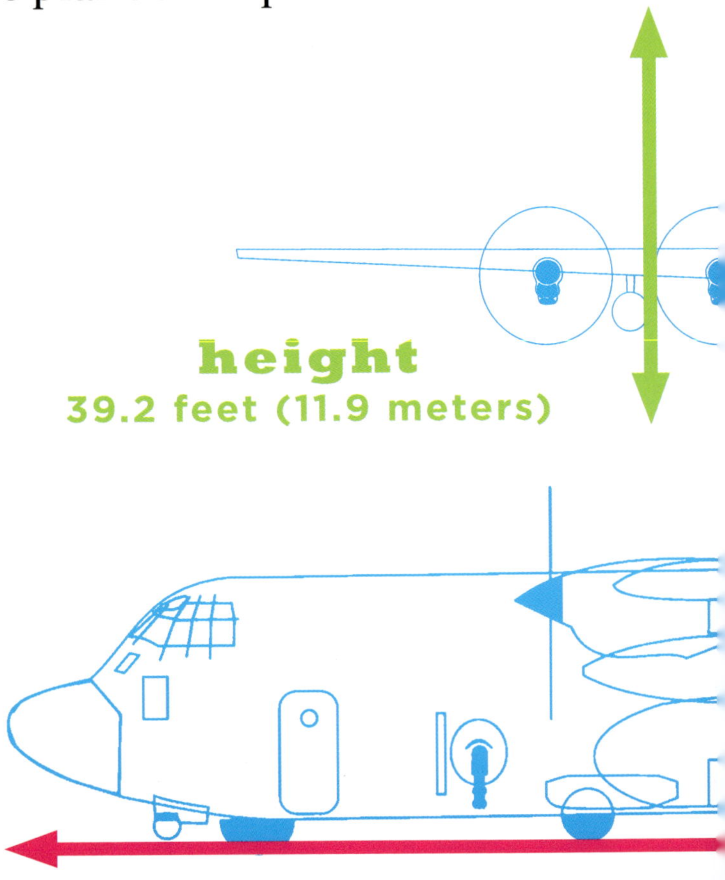

GHOSTRIDER STATS

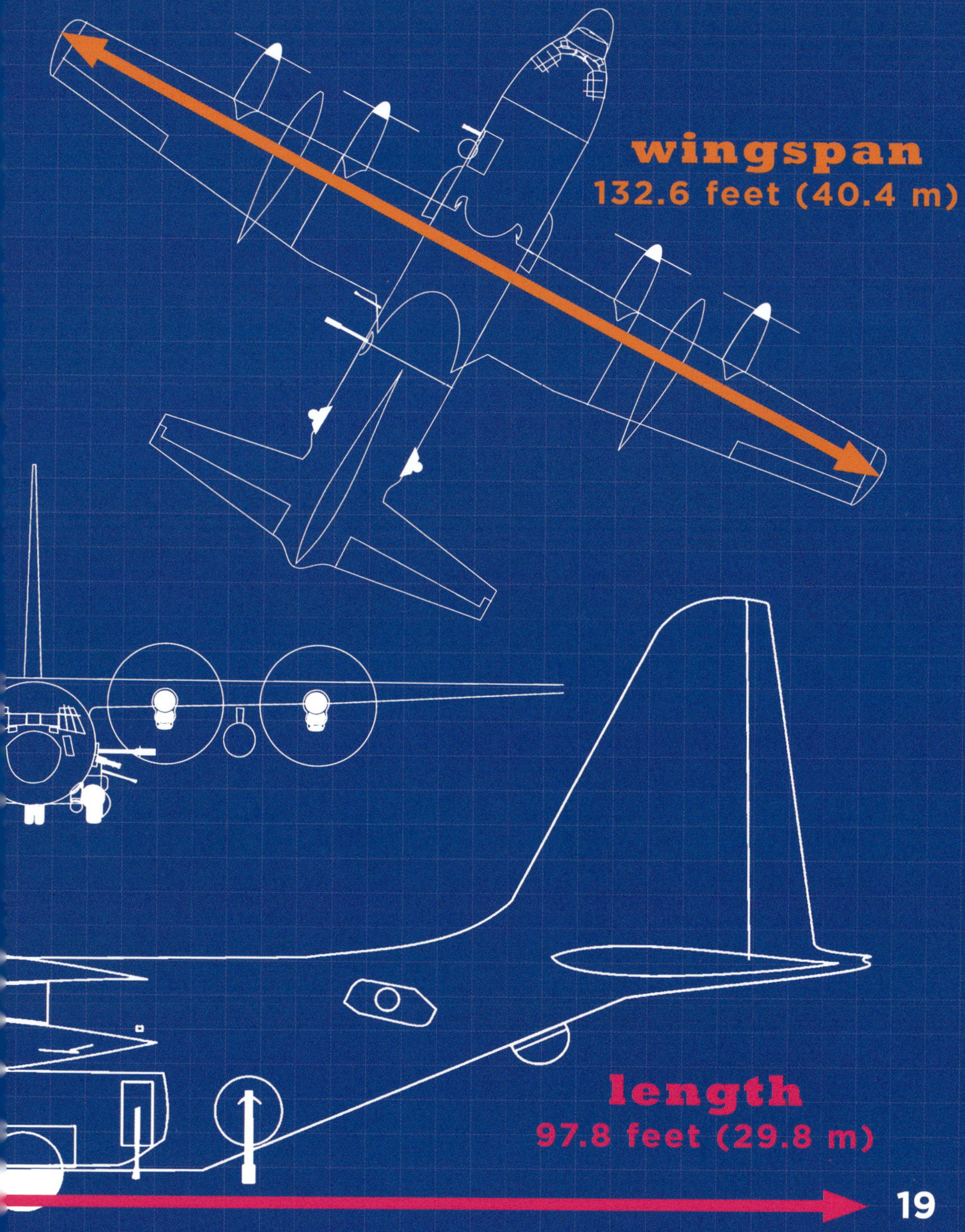

GHOSTRIDER PARTS

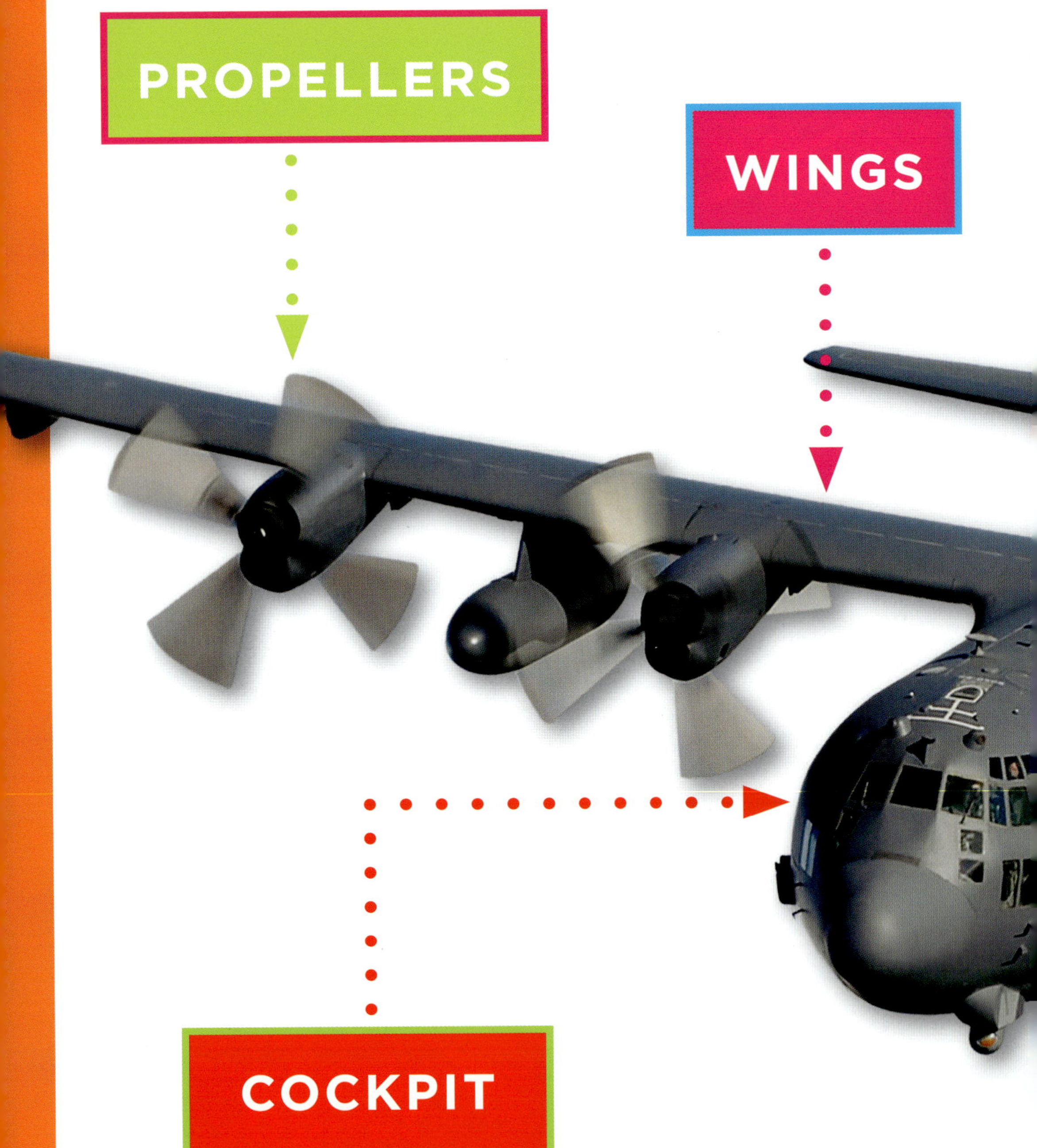

CARGO BAY
CANNONS

CHAPTER 4

The Ghostrider in ACTION

The Ghostrider will support U.S. soldiers around the world. It can fly low to the ground. The plane's weapons will take out enemies.

Gathering Information

The Ghostrider will also gather information. Pilots will fly it over enemy lands. The plane then sends information to ground soldiers. Ghostriders will also help in search and rescue missions.

The U.S. Air Force expects to have 37 Ghostriders in action by 2023.

BY THE NUMBERS

9
number of crew members needed

4

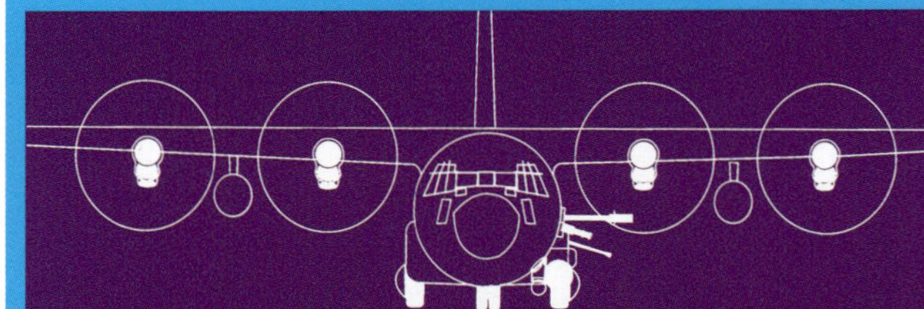

NUMBER OF ENGINES

28,000 feet
(8,534 m)
MAXIMUM FLYING HEIGHT

416
miles (669 km) per hour

TOP SPEED

$115 MILLION
cost to build one Ghostrider

Mission Support

The Ghostrider carries a lot of firepower. This gunship swoops into action at a moment's notice. It will support missions for years to come.

GLOSSARY

cannon (KAN-uhn)—a large, heavy gun that fires explosives

combat (kahm-BAT)—active fighting, often in a war

detect (dee-TEKT)—to discover the existence or presence of something

GPS—a system used to find the location of something on Earth

missile (MIS-uhl)—a weapon that can be thrown or projected to hit an object far away

radar (RAY-dar)—a device that sends out radio waves for finding the location and speed of a moving object

sensor (SEN-sor)—a device that finds heat, light, sound, motion, or other things

Vietnam War (vee-uht-NAHM WAHR)—a conflict between North Vietnam and South Vietnam that lasted between 1954 and 1975

LEARN MORE

BOOKS

Boothroyd, Jennifer. *Inside the US Air Force*. US Armed Forces. Minneapolis: Lerner Publications, 2018.

Garstecki, Julia. *Military Aircraft*. Military Tech. Mankato, MN: Black Rabbit Books, 2018.

Peterson, Judy Monroe. *All about Planes*. Transportation. New York: Britannica Educational Publishing in association with Rosen Educational Services, 2017.

WEBSITES

AC-130J Ghostrider
www.af.mil/About-Us/Fact-Sheets/Display/Article/467756/ac-130j-ghostrider/

See the USAF's Newest Gunship
www.cnn.com/videos/us/2015/11/21/ac130j-ghostrider-gunship-orig-bb-vstan.cnn

U.S. Air Force's Gunship, Ghostrider, Is Almost Ready for Combat
www.youtube.com/watch?v=1FYiQ53CSCs

INDEX